the life-changing magic of piling things up

the American art of cluttering and hoarding

katrina karapandi with jason liller

MILLHANDS PRESS

Published by **Millhands Press**

PO Box 162, Mechanicsburg, PA 17055

ISBN 978-0-9989205-2-8

Printed in the United States of America

Contents

Contents

Introduction

I hated Mollie Ackerman. She was always one step ahead of me, always more popular than I was, always a little better at everything. Better at English and math, better at sports, better at clothes and makeup. Better with boys. When I strutted into class with my shiny new Trapper Keeper binder, she whipped out a custom-designed Gloria Vanderbilt personal organizer. When I wore hand-me-down Toughskin corduroys, she showed up in sprayed-on, sequin-studded Jordache jeans. When Greg Trescott took me to the prom, he spent the evening dancing with Mollie while I ate all the food on the refreshment table. Jerk.

I was jealous of Mollie in pretty much every way imaginable. I have especially vivid memories of her Hawaiian vacation. Well, not first-hand memories. That would be impossible because I wasn't there. I was in Hoboken enjoying the Hudson waterfront while she basked in the sun and sand of glamorous Waikiki. And how did her family pay for that trip? By selling her dad's old comic books and baseball cards. They traded a bunch of packed-away things that Mr. Ackerman hadn't thought about in years for a first-class family trip to Hawaii.

When I bitterly told my own dad about Mollie's fantasy vacation, his grimace betrayed the profound pain of a man who is well acquainted with regret. He said, "I had a huge collection of old comic books and baseball cards, but *my mother threw it all away.*"

No kidding. You can't finance a vacation with valuables that are buried in a landfill.

There's a lesson to be learned here: **Stop getting rid of things.** And I'm not talking about bona fide trash; for God's sake, get rid of those dirty diapers and used menstrual goodies. No, I'm talking about the magazines, the newspapers, the fast-food gewgaws, the childhood toys, and all the knick-knacky things that friends and family always pester you to throw out. Don't do it. You have the room. And even if you think you don't, you do. That's what the trunk of the car and the space behind the couch are for.

Friends may come and friends may go, but stuff is always with you

Don't let anyone kid you: Life is all about accumulating stuff. There is an insidious movement afoot to convince us that having less stuff helps us live simpler lives. *Declutter* and *minimize* are buzzwords polluting the lexicon as millions of Americans cast aside their hard-earned possessions in a misguided quest for peace and serenity. **I don't work my ass off so that I can have less stuff, and neither should you.**

The noble lineage of piling things up

Anyone who grew up during the Great Depression understands a fundamental truth about throwing things away: It's a bad idea. Since World War II ended we've built what has famously been called a "disposable society." It isn't a badge of honor. No other civilization has been so quick and so eager to cast off its material components. Reverse the trend. Keep your stuff.

Accumulation is good for the environment

Decluttering doesn't do any favors to your local landfill. It is the responsibility of each of us, as environmentally conscious global citizens, to keep our possessions right where they belong: in our homes. You spent good money on your stuff. **Stuff equals money and your house is the bank. Fill it up!**

Accumulation is good for the economy

And speaking of global citizenship, in today's interconnected economy, buying less stuff could be crippling. There are entire cities in China devoted to the manufacture of the awesome goods that patiently sit on shelves at the dollar store just waiting for us to give them loving homes. Do you want to contribute to a new global recession? Of course not. Do your bit and buy more stuff.

Accumulation is good for the soul

Does Bill Gates have full cabinets? Does Donald Trump have a packed trophy case? Does Elon Musk have a loaded closet? You better believe it. When Jed Clampett struck oil on his mountain homestead in *The Beverly Hillbillies* he didn't celebrate by emptying out the root cellar. Hell no. He went shopping. Jed lived an uncluttered lifestyle long enough to understand something that the smugly decluttered hipsters have yet to grasp: **Having stuff is better than the alternative.**

Take it from Jed: Acquisition is the root of all happiness. Nothing beats the satisfaction of looking around the house, patting yourself on the back, and saying, "Yep, it's all mine." If there's something missing in your life, if there's a yawning emptiness that you can't put your finger on, or if there's a gnawing dissatisfaction eating away at your soul, it's time to fill the void. And nothing fills a void like material possessions. It's a fact. Ask anyone who's run out of closet space.

You can't have it all: intelligent accumulation

My husband likes to bring home carloads of junk, and I don't like to get rid of anything. This makes us a world-class house-filling couple, but thanks to me we don't suck up every piece of whatever-it-is that crosses our path. Far from it. I preach the gospel of *Intelligent Accumulation.* Accumulation should have a point to it. It isn't enough to be a trash magnet; there has to be a purpose to what you do. And given that we all (well, most of us) only have a limited amount of space to fill, it's also essential that you do a little thinking before jumping into major high-volume commitments.

Here's an example: The contents of a nearby resort hotel that had closed a few years back were being auctioned off. This is exactly the sort of trap that my husband is powerless to resist. On the day of the auction he placed a few foolhardy bids and became the proud new owner of several industrial dishwasher trays filled with mismatched drinking glasses (I swear that no two of them are alike), three fold-up hard-surface table covers that are too big for any tabletop in our house, and one entire hotel room. Yes, he won *an entire hotel room* at the auction. Everything in the room was his, *including* the things that were nailed down, and he had to take possession of it all, right down to the toilet and the shower fixtures. He could have taken the wallpaper if he had wanted to strip it off (thank God he didn't).

When he told me what he had done I nearly burst into flame right there in the kitchen. I said there was no way were taking all of that crap. There are better things to fill the cavities in our home than institutional blackout curtains, an old 1990s TV, and a toilet that's been sat on by the butts of 10,000 strangers. Can you imagine what's been in that thing? With fires of rage shooting from my eyes I said that there was exactly one thing in that room that might be worth owning and that I was willing to take and that was the safe. *It was broken.* So, in other words, total loss. And that's when he told me what his M.O. had been: "We can use the mattress to replace the old one in the guest room!"

WHAT WAS HE THINKING? Sure we can use the old hotel mattress—right after we burn the impurities out of it in the town incinerator. This was a classic example of my husband catching bargain fever, except that none of the things that he bought was a bargain. On the contrary, this adventure was a total loss and I will never let him forget it (because that's how I roll). If he had kept his wits about him, and not got swept up in the romance of owning a shower curtain that I can guarantee would look like a Jackson Pollock painting under UV light, he could have saved himself all of the harassment that I dish out to him at every opportunity. "Yes, that lawn mower is a bargain. *Just like that damn hotel room that you bought.*"

Here's another example of ignoring the principle of Intelligent Accumulation: I use a lot of printer paper. Once, when I was nearly out and needed more, my husband decided to solve my paper deficits once and for all. He visited an auction of surplus merchandise (I swear he can't stay away) and placed a bid, which he naturally won, on a pallet of printer paper. Ladies and gentlemen, we are talking about forty cases of printer paper stacked in a cube almost five feet tall (and I'm only four-foot-nine!). Two-thousand pounds of paper. That's a ton. One solid ton of paper. 200,000 sheets. Enough to go to the Moon and back probably. Plus one wooden pallet.

As nice as it was of him to think about my professional needs, I gently told him that there was no way in hell that we could store forty cases of paper in our already bursting-at-the-seams home. He promised that we'd find a solution and we set off to claim our prize. Imagine my delight when, upon entering the warehouse where the auction merchandise awaited its proud new owners, I was faced with a colossal pallet of continuous-feed printer paper. This is the type of paper that's attached end-to-end and folds up like an accordion, the type of paper that has hole-punched perforated strips on the sides, the type of paper that *no one has used in their homes in over a generation.* And we had a ton of it.

He may as well have bought a pallet of flash bulbs for a digital camera. Once again, just like the hotel room, we had to dispose of a massive white elephant that we couldn't unload for love or money. If only he had inspected his quarry a bit before placing that impulsive bid. Oh, well. At least I got a good story out of it. And maybe he's learned his lesson. Or maybe he hasn't.

Intelligent Accumulation means exactly what it says. It means thinking before you buy. It means asking yourself if you will actually use what you purchase, if it holds meaning for you, if it makes you happy, if it makes sense, if you have *room* for it. Maybe you live in a warehouse. If so, lucky you. Most of us don't and, for us, space is a very real issue. Therefore, it also means managing space and prioritizing acquisitions. Accumulate intelligently.

Don't be like my husband. Be like me. Accumulate intelligently. Unless your home is like the TARDIS on *Doctor Who* (bigger on the inside), you can't afford to lose precious space to useless clutter when there's so much *good* clutter that still needs a loving home.

1

—

Your house is not your home

The first step on your life-changing journey of piling things up is to challenge some fundamental attitudes about your home that you've probably carried around for decades. Most of us are conditioned to believe that our houses are where we build our lives and raise our families, where we gather for meals and rest our heads. Of course you can do all of these things in your house, but every class-A accumulator knows that *your house is not your home.* Your house is a place to keep your things, and the living that goes on around and among your possessions is strictly incidental. Pull the car out of the garage. You're going to need the space.

The method of intelligent accumulation

Step one: Reduce your footprint

How much space does a person need? How much room do you actually require to live your life?

Probably very little. That leaves plenty of room for all of your things.

The kitchen

How much space do you need in your kitchen? Since the kitchen is where you allegedly cook, it's important to keep the classic food-prep triangle (the space between the refrigerator, the sink, and the stove) clear. Also, storing things on the range top or inside the oven is potentially problematic (my genius husband once stashed some plastic storage containers in the oven. I found this out the hard way and, believe me, it was a mess that a can of *Easy-Off Heavy Duty Oven Cleaner* was powerless to mop up).

The best way to maximize your kitchen storage is to avoid using the kitchen. My cooking is pretty much limited to the simple things: I make a smashing batch of Kraft Macaroni & Cheese, I whip up a bowl of Kellogg's Froot Loops with brilliant *savoir faire,* and my Hamburger Helper brings all the boys to the TV tray. The common denominator here is that nothing that I do

15

in the kitchen requires much space. Just a couple of square feet will do. That leaves plenty of room on the kitchen counter for my roller blades.

The living room and the dining room

How much space do you need in your living room? Enough to get from the front door to the couch, and enough to have an unobstructed view of the TV. That's it. And the dining room, unless you think you live in Downton Abbey, is irrelevant.

The real-estate programs that suck up hours of my time every day are filled with bright young couples who demand homes with *open-concept floor plans*. I prefer houses that are divided into rooms, but that's just me. One benefit of open concept, though, is that It provides lots of space for stuff. When we lived in a 700-square-foot cottage we had toys and books piled up along the walls, and our living space was pared down to a couch, a dining-room table, and a narrow passage between them. Now that we have a much larger home, we have even more places to pile things up.

The bedroom

How much space do you need in your bedroom? Enough to get to your bed and to your closet (unless you leave your clothes piled on the floor). If you're single you can even use some of your bedspace to store linens and such.

Cavernous master suites are all the rage nowadays. Do people spend their whole lives in their bedrooms? I use mine for sleeping (believe me, there's nothing *else* going on in there), and maybe for getting dressed. If I had the spacious retreat that so many of my fellow TV-viewers clearly crave I would have an expansive space for a much larger wardrobe. Room for more shoes and clothes? Maybe a spacious master suite isn't such a bad idea after all. As it is, I have enough room in bed for me and my dog and my husband. Any other unoccupied space is wasted storage.

The bathroom

How much space do you need in your bathroom? Enough to get to the shower and the sink and the toilet (basically anything that spits water) and enough elbow room to get to the toilet paper without knocking anything over.

Otherwise, the bathroom is where things get interesting. There are a number of items that we use exclusively (or nearly so) in the bathroom: towels, toiletries, *People* magazine. I like to keep plenty of reading material within arm's reach of the toilet, and it's gratifying to see bathroom space that would otherwise be wasted filled with the finest gossip rags that money can buy. Just be sure to keep your glossy treasures clear of your husband's splash radius.

Empty nest? Full room!

Among the countless reasons to look forward to your children leaving home (assuming they ever do) is all the extra space you'll capture the moment they step across that threshold into the cold cruel world. I filled my daughter's room within twenty-four hours of shipping her off to college and I never looked back. I'm not saying there won't be some wailing and gnashing of teeth when she comes home for a visit, but she's an adult now. She can take it.

Step two: Get comfortable with accumulation

While many of us are thankfully blessed with a natural tendency to accumulate, there are many more who, sadly, are predisposed to toss out what they wrongly assume to be trash.

Getting comfortable with accumulation is mostly a simple matter of perspective. Is that candy wrapper that you thoughtlessly threw away really a waste product? Or is it a treasured souvenir of an after-work jaunt to the grocery store? That cereal box that you put in the recycle bin may be a priceless relic of the very last time that you got to enjoy that particular brand of breakfast goodness. I think fondly of the discontinued cereals of my youth—Freakies, Waffelos, Crispy Wheats 'n Raisins, Sir Grapefellow—and wish that I had saved those boxes so they could take me back to youthful Saturday mornings on the living-room floor, cereal bowl in hand, watching *H.R. Pufnstuf* and *Scooby-Doo*.

I know a guy named Ezekiel who saves pretty much everything he touches. At night he places each object that he collected that day into a Ziploc bag carefully labeled with date, location, and a brief description of the item's significance. I once watched him get weepy over a carefully conserved wetnap that had wiped birthday-cake icing from his face on the day he turned ten years old. It was enough to inspire the most hardcore hoarder to hoard even harder.

Now you might think that Ezekiel's home is a disgusting, unsanitary mess, but nothing could be further from the truth. Everything is scrupulously well organized, arranged by an arcane method known only to its creator, kept reasonably clean and dust-free, and stacked so that he can get to the kitchen, the bathroom, and the mattress (which is walled in on three-and-a-half sides by stacks of old phone books). Truth be told, even I thought he had gone a bit too far, but when he showed me a napkin from his visit to the Tastee-Freez after seeing *Jaws* for the first time in 1975, my heart went all aflutter and, well, he made me a believer. Which brings me to step three.

Step three: Accumulate with purpose

Ezekiel doesn't pile things up out of a shallow desire to fill space or because he has some pathological fear of letting things go. He does it because he's made a commitment to archive his life. Any object to which he can attach any degree of importance finds its way into his home where it is enshrined for eternity. He doesn't keep used toilet paper, though. That would be gross. Instead, he documents his soiled Charmin with photographs, a proclivity that used to cause problems in public restrooms before the era of silent cell-phone cameras. The sounds of clicking shutters and advancing film got him more than one date with local law enforcement personnel. Luckily for him, the most trouble he ever got into was a stern warning, carefully given at arm's length, to refrain from snapping photos in the john. Now I'm no attorney, but I don't think that admonition was legally enforceable, and neither did Ezekiel, who couldn't bear to leave his leavings unrecorded, making him something of a minor celebrity in police departments across the nation.

But we're getting tastelessly off track. The point here is that there is a point to what Ezekiel does. There's a method to his madness. He maintains a house filled with tangible links to his past. As for me, my weaknesses are media: books, movies, and music. I'm a researcher by nature. Anything that comes up, any question that anyone asks, I'm hitting the books looking for answers. I demand comprehensive collections and I will never have enough to make me happy. If there's a book that I need or an album that I want to listen to, I want to be able to put my hands on it without leaving the house. Notice that I said I want to be able to *put my hands on it*. No digital stuff. Downloading and streaming don't cut it. There's something comforting and reassuring about the tangible permanence of a physical object that can't be matched by putting stuff "in the cloud."

What do *you* collect? What do find yourself unable to part with? What do you pile up?

Step four: Own it and don't look back

And I mean *own* it. **Harness your inner grabby hands and get busy.** Your friends will tell you you're nuts, your family will stage interventions, your out-of-town relatives will no longer visit, and your coworkers will probably be blissfully unaware, but YOU will rest easy, secure in the knowledge that you have a houseload of cool stuff and that all the haters are secretly jealous of your massive inventory. **Kiss your extra space goodbye. It's time to start piling things up!**

2

Clothes and shoes

When we bought our new home we picked one with the sort of palatial master-bedroom suite that people gush over on those real-estate shows that keep Aunt Judy plastered to her La-Z-Boy recliner eighteen hours a day. Our master bedroom is the size of a small European country, which is an awful lot of space for a room that's used only for sleeping, getting dressed, and other things that I'm told are supposed to happen in bedrooms.

When I have space, I fill it. The walk-in closet was enough for a little while. I even shared it with my husband, who complained that his stuff was being squeezed into an ever-smaller fraction of the left hangar bar before giving up and taking his measly handful of shirts to the garage where he stores them with the tools. Once the closet was exclusively mine I really maximized its potential. I piled clothes wide and deep across every square foot until they poured out of the closet and into the bedroom, which meant that the closet door was stuck in the "open" position which, in turn, meant that there was a sliver of wasted space between the door and the wall. When my husband went to the garage to fetch a golf shirt, I told him to bring me back a hammer and a screwdriver. A few whacks later and that door was off its hinges for good. No more wasted space.

Now that my wardrobe was no longer confined to the closet, it was free to roam across the floor into a glorious landscape of blue-denim mountains and dirty-sock hills. I could break the surface at any point and see clothing stratified just like the ancient silt layers visible on the walls of the Grand Canyon.

Clothes are the easiest things to store, but it's hard to keep them wrinkle-free and ready-to-wear. **I ease my storage burden by focusing on building a wardrobe of outfits that are forgiving of rough treatment.** I recommend sweatpants, pajamas, and t-shirts—clothes that represent the pinnacle of comfort, yet can be wadded up and shoved in every nook and cranny without affecting their wearability. This can solve your storage problems, cut down on household labor, and put you on the cutting edge of discount-store couture in one single stroke.

Clothes that are out of style

When it comes to storing older outfits, I recommend the archive system: sort your outfits by decade, then store them in labeled plastic bins. This comes in way handy if you aren't shy about being two or more decades out of style. If I love the night life and want to boogie on the disco round, I just dip into my '70s collection for a glitter-sequined, off-the-shoulder number. If I feel like hanging at the mall or going to the arcade for some Pac-Man, I open my '80s boxes for a bright, bold, angular outfit. And if I'm in a glum and oh-so-serious mood I can crack open a '90s box for some authentic vintage flannel and torn jeans.

I also have vast swaths of wardrobe organized by color, a resplendent fashion rainbow. If it's Aunt Martha's funeral, Maria's quinceañera, or the St. Patrick's Day beerfest down at the Knights of Columbus hall, I know just the hue to wear and exactly where I'll find it.

Maybe you're challenged more by storage than by organization. If so, no worries. **The great thing about clothes is that they can be squashed really, really flat.** Get yourself a pizza peel (a giant wooden spatula for lifting pizzas out of hot ovens) and a muscular friend. Stack some folded clothes on the floor in the closet, or in the middle of the room if you like, until they reach the ceiling. Then have your friend use the pizza peel to compress the clothes—with all his might!—while you stack more on top. Extract the peel and repeat the process until the layers of clothes are packed so tightly that not even a butter knife could be jammed between them. Now you have a solid column of clothes from floor to ceiling. If you need something from the middle of that stack, though, you'll have to figure it out yourself.

Clothes that don't fit

I know you've heard it a million times: *Don't keep clothes that no longer fit.* If you are ever a size four again (ha ha) you can buy all new clothes. What these "experts" don't tell you is that you will never be a size four again so you'll never have the opportunity to build a new size-four wardrobe. Keeping those old clothes, and putting them where you can see them, will motivate you to lose weight. Anyone who tells you otherwise is either working for the clothing industry *(spend money on new clothes; don't keep your old ones!)* or working for the food industry *(keep eating and stay fat!)*. **Your**

old clothes will remind you and encourage you to lose weight. *Go to the gym!* they shout. *Wear us again!* they plead.

Or at least that's the idea. I keep all of my old clothes and I know the motivation will kick in any time now. I'll diet and exercise like I mean it. I'll once again slink around in my acid-washed jeans and Def Leppard T-shirt and it'll all be because I kept those thirty-year-old clothes that everyone thought I should trash. I'm still looking forward to it.

Kids' clothes

It breaks my heart when parents truck their kid's clothes to the thrift store after they've outgrown them. Most people save a few special outfits, and that's great, but I say that *all* of the outfits are special. **How can you bear to part with a shirt that has ketchup stains from your kid's first Happy Meal?** Or the torn pants from the first climb over the crib rail? Only a heartless so-and-so could dispose of such treasures. And if you have hoarder's remorse you can assuage your regret by reminding yourself that your grown children may choose to clothe their own offspring with their hand-me-downs (of course they won't because they don't want to deprive themselves of the shopping opportunities that come with having a kid, but if telling yourself that gets you through the rough spots, then do it early and often).

Pro tips

I spent years wading through a knee-deep layer of clothes that I spent good money on. I even sorted them into sectors by type: jeans in the corner, blouses under the air conditioner, t-shirts in front of the closet (which was already packed solid floor-to-ceiling), underwear on the foot of the bed, bras hanging from the ceiling fan... you get the idea. After a while, though, this got to be a bit much even for me. I knew that I had to find a way to archive my wardrobe.

Clothes are soft and squishy and you can pack a lot of them into a tiny space. Vacuum bags are lifesavers. I'm talking about those large plastic bags with vacuum-hose hookups that you can buy at the low-end discount stores. Shove as many clothes as you can into the bag, suck out all the air, and *voilà!* A whole wad of clothes in an itty-bitty bag.

I once bought a batch of storage bags, opened one up, poured in a load of clothes, and stomped away like I was squashing grapes in Bordeaux. I smashed those clothes flatter than Mollie Ackerman's skinny white ass, piled on another load, and stomped some more. It's a good thing I lived in a ground-floor apartment.

I filled the bag to several times its design capacity, hooked up the vacuum and sucked out the air. When I was done that thing was packed as tight as my 1984 Jordache jeans. Perfect. But I had failed to anticipate the tremendous weight of a closet full of clothes compressed down to the size of a beer cooler. It was like having the core of a black hole right there on my bedroom floor, an object so dense it probably affected the tides. Simply put, there was no way this bag of clothing was leaving the room and I sure as hell wasn't going to unload it. I did the only sensible thing: I put a cushion on it and turned it into an ottoman.

My friend Ezekiel, who can always be counted upon for ingenious storage innovation, took this process a step further. He rigged up an old kitchen trash compactor with a vacuum-cleaner connection. Then he used the compactor to compress the bag into a tiny little cube and simultaneously sucked out all of the air with the vacuum cleaner. Now he has a whole room filled with dense, rock-hard clothing bags stacked like bricks and it is amazing to behold.

Shoes

I love shoes. I still remember that day in the '80s when Mollie Ackerman wore neon-yellow pumps to school. I needed those shoes more than men need football and she had no business wearing them if I couldn't have them. She got off the school bus and stepped ankle-deep in dog poop. Who would think that such a simple thing could make me the happiest girl on the planet?

But enough about Mollie. I have one of those popular cubby-hole shoe-storage systems in my closet.

Each receptacle is designed to hold one pair, but I've managed to make them accommodate between two and five pairs depending upon the type of shoe. So my wall is filled with untold numbers of shoes, but I have far more footwear than the storage system can handle. And, unlike most clothing, shoes cannot be folded or wadded up. Given this, and the fact that I truly believe that shoes should be kept wherever I choose to remove them, there is a sea of shoes all over the floor of my closet, pouring out into the bedroom, piled up at the foot of the bed, shoved into the corners of the living room and kitchen, and in a respectable mound in the foyer where they are the first things company sees when they come in the front door. Out-of-season winter footwear gets pitched into the mud room and the basement.

The greatest problem with unorganized shoe storage is the proliferation of unmatched shoes. It's such a drag when you're running late and you can only find one shoe of a pair and NO other pair will do. Here's how to cope with the drama:

1). Accuse your husband of losing the shoe.

2). Accuse your daughter of wearing the shoe.

3). Make your husband and your daughter scour the house in search of the shoe.

4). Buy new shoes.

So my massive shoe inventory is really a function of my husband's and daughter's shortcomings. But I have to say, in spite of their inability to locate the shoes that they lost, I really appreciate the fact that they try. And that they're careful not to damage any of the many shoes that they have to wade through throughout the house as they search.

My husband doesn't understand how one person can have so many shoes. He criticizes and bemoans and grumbles, but I don't understand how one man can get by with only two pairs. That's it. That's all he's got. One pair of tennis shoes and one pair of "good" shoes (and the latter he purchased under duress). He doesn't even know what he's talking about! **How is someone who owns exactly two pairs of shoes qualified to discuss shoe ownership?** Go buy another 150 pairs and then I'll listen to what you have to say.

3

Books

Anyone who knows me knows that I love books. I always wanted a library in my home, a room dedicated to books and reading, the walls lined with shelves, and an easy chair where I could spend quiet hours with favorite authors. Sadly, I never got the library I wanted, but I did get more books than I ever could have imagined, and I filled my home with them. That's when it hit me: *My home is my library!* And why should I limit myself to storing books only on bookshelves? How boring. While there's nothing sadder than using bookshelves to display things other than books (bookshelves are not for knick-knacks!), the fact is that books don't belong exclusively on bookshelves. They belong in every corner of the house and believe me, I've proven this through extensive real-world experience. I have stacked books on every surface, including what precious little empty floor space was still available.

Book lovers share a common philosophy that once a book joins the collection it is a permanent member of the family, never to be abandoned or cast away. Back in the dark ages, when I was suckered into a temporary (thank God) nightmare of decluttering, I disposed of many books. It was heartbreaking and I still suffer traumatic flashbacks of giving away precious copies of *The Official Preppy Handbook, 101 Uses for a Dead Cat,* and *Real Men Don't Eat Quiche.* In the years since, I've comforted myself with the knowledge that those books are now changing lives in someone else's home. And as painful as it may have been to divest myself of those volumes, it allowed me to experience the joy of reacquiring lost titles and welcoming them back into the fold. There's only one thing better than getting a new book and that's getting it all over again!

Fast-forward to today. Books cram every room of my home and then some. I love it when people drop by and marvel at the breadth and scope of my collection, exclaiming over the range of erudite topics favored by their hostess, and *maybe* just a little overwhelmed by the sheer volume of volumes on display.

Except that almost never happens. When I have company (which is rare because company means cleaning the house—*as if*), my guests walk right past the books like they aren't even there. They don't even pause to scan the spines, and that really pisses me off. I was going to put a bookshelf right inside the front door facing the entrance so that visitors would have no choice but to confront the books. The books would literally be in their faces. If I had my way, that bookshelf would be so close to the front door that visitors would have to sidestep to get around it. Sadly, I *didn't* get my way because my husband vetoed this scheme, but one day he'll be in New Jersey on business and there'll be a big booky surprise waiting for him right inside the front door when he returns.

Now maybe books aren't your thing, and filling your home with bound wood pulp doesn't ring your bell. I won't look down on you too much for feeling that way, but it's important to remember that **books make you look smart, and if you have a lot of them your friends will overestimate your intelligence** and start asking for advice about things that you know nothing about. Case in point: My friend Roxanne, who I can pretty much guarantee hasn't cracked a book since high school, was whining about how she couldn't make a frozen margarita because her crusty forty-year-old blender was on the fritz. She listened while I droned on at length about the inner workings of her grimy avocado-green 1978-model Osterizer and why it might have stopped working. I had no idea what I was talking about, but that didn't stop me from yakking, nor did it prevent Roxanne from basking in the rosy glow of my boundless authority. After all, I read lots of books, right? I must be smart. You may say I'm a fraud, but can I help it if people think I'm an expert? About forty-five minutes into this masquerade Roxanne called my bluff: could I *fix* her blender? For a brief moment I imagined my life as the mythical *Blender Mender,* the inspiring heroine of kitchen-appliance folklore, itinerant enabler of yucky vegetable smoothies and high-effort boozy concoctions. Then I came to terms with my utter lack of mechanical aptitude and realized that my improvised technoramble had backed me into a corner. I poked at the thing for a minute and delivered the bad news: Her beloved blender had made its last margarita. I told her to get a new one and soon, because I like margaritas but I'm too lazy to make them. This was my expert opinion. I sure as hell wasn't giving her *my* 1978 Osterizer.

A library custom-built to intimidate

While I encourage you to pack books into every available space, I also urge you to think about which books you put where. My sister has a massive bookshelf in her living room filled with the classics of Western literature, and I'm not talking about the easy ones you read in high school. She has shelf upon shelf of Roman poets, renaissance science, and untranslated Proust. Anyone who scans her bookshelf knows instantly that she's the smartest person in the room—an advantage that she never fails to exploit.

What her guests don't see is her secret bedroom bookcase. If they were to stumble into her boudoir they'd find shelf after shelf polluted with Harlequin romances and *Twilight* novels. Now I'm not saying that she doesn't read the books on the front-room shelves; on the contrary, I know for a fact that she does. The key is that she placed them where her guests would see them (Why do her guests pay attention to books and mine don't? I obviously need different guests), and now they all think she's some kind of genius. *Untranslated Proust.* Seriously.

Packing 'em in

When a shelf is filled to capacity, and you are completely out of space, here's a sure-fire way to cram in one more volume: Use a putty knife or a crowbar to spread two of the books apart just a little bit and then hammer in a new one with a rubber mallet. Just make sure you have no immediate plans to read any of the books on that shelf because you might have to take the whole damn thing apart to remove them.

I am loath to warn against overpacking anything (*overpacked* pretty much sums me up), but if your bookshelves are freestanding, like the build-it-yourself cheapies that they sell at Walmart, beware of filling them beyond the manufacturer's recommended load. If the sidewalls start to bow outward there's a chance that the whole thing will pop apart like a badly managed Jenga tower. The best way to defuse this situation is to pack even more books into the bookcase. That way, even if the thing flies apart like a squeezed deck of playing cards, the books will, with any luck, stay intact. It's like filling a mold: if the books are packed in tightly enough you can peel away the sides without causing a calamity.

There is a flaw in this strategy, though, and that's that the books themselves become structural. If you decide to chisel out that copy of *Thin Thighs in 30 Days* that you've been ignoring for the past quarter century, you may risk bringing the whole enterprise tumbling down around your feet. And books are *heavy*. You don't generally want them cascading down like Niagara. You could avoid the whole issue by buying a new copy of *Thin Thighs in 30 Days* and leaving the old one where it is. I mean, what's one more book, right?

On the other hand, sometimes a calamity is good. A foundation-shaking book avalanche blew the lid off of my nephew's slick scheme to abscond to the bathroom with my 1972 copy of *The Joy of Sex*—a book that saw more action at the bottom of a 200-pound pile of books than it ever did in my bedroom. Despite his shame at being discovered, the book still vanished a few weeks later and, to this day, he is the prime suspect. Oh well; at least someone's getting some use out of it.

Where I draw the line

At this point, it should go without saying that I'm a big fan of accumulating things. It's rewarding to have a bunch of stuff laying around and being able to say, "I did this!" But I draw the line at jars filled with pocket lint and grocery bags packed with used tissues. That's just gross. And I also don't recommend collecting *Reader's Digest Condensed Books* or old *National Geographics*.

You've seen *Reader's Digest Condensed Books*. They're little hardcover editions that contain the text of four or five books, but with all of the juice squeezed out of them. For decades, editors at *Reader's Digest* went through contemporary bestsellers, wrung out everything that didn't seem important, along with all of the sex scenes and cuss words, and then crammed four or five newly condensed books into a single slim volume. *That's* how much stuff they cut out. The bindings are designed to look "elegant" in a white-bread 1960s kind of way, but their design only makes them easy to identify, even from a distance—and that's not a good thing. The visiting book snobs won't like it. Toss those and get the real, uncondensed books. They'll look better on your shelf and they'll still have all the sex scenes and cuss words that *Reader's Digest* sliced out. In other words, they will no longer be sanitized for your protection. They'll still have the good parts (Note to *Reader's Digest:* How about a series of books that contain only the expurgated sex scenes?). Even better: If you replace every volume of your *Reader's Digest Condensed Books* with copies of the actual books that *RD* sliced and diced, then you'll instantly have four or five new books for every *Reader's Digest* book that you pitch. That's a serious net gain of books. It's a triumph of quality *and* quantity. Who wouldn't be okay with that?

If you really feel the need to keep those bowdlerized *Reader's Digest* editions, I'll grant exemptions to those who feel a nostalgic pang because Aunt Ruth used to keep a stack of them on the end table in her den. If this is you, you're off the hook.

National Geographic and other silliness

Unlike *Reader's Digest Condensed Books*, no one impugns the quality of *National Geographic* (though I hold that it ain't what it used to be). And yes, I know they're not books, but they're close enough, and I couldn't be bothered to write a whole chapter about magazines.

The basements of America are loaded with stacks of moldy *NatGeos* which raises the question: When did we decide that this magazine was too good to throw out along with last month's *Better Homes and Gardens?* Probably about the same time that thirteen-year-old boys discovered that *National Geographic*, with almost suspicious regularity, published photos of bare-chested women. If you were a young boy, and Dad's stack of *Playboys* was off limits (and likely didn't officially exist), *National Geographic* was readily available. And it was educational! At least that's what Mom told herself with a worried brow while Johnny lingered a little too long on that one page…

National G, as my husband likes to call it, also came with cool fold-up maps and occasionally other supplemental goodies like *flexidiscs,* floppy phonograph records that could be bound into magazines, given away in cereal boxes, etc. My favorite *National Geographic* one was "Songs of the Humpback Whale" in which the narrator pronounced the *WH* in "whale" with such a whoosh that it practically blew my hair back. But without an old phonograph, that flexidisc is useless. It's a good thing you saved your old record player. *Right?*

Years ago, *National Geographic* came out with a big CD-ROM set of its entire printed output. I viewed this as an insidious attempt to get us to clean out our cellars, but I must admit that it made it a lot easier to access decades of articles from a journal that had been publishing since 1888 (no word, though, on whether the search engine made it easier to find the topless photos upon which the magazine built its reputation).

Mad Magazine did the same thing: Every issue was committed to a shiny silvery disc and put before the public. A friend sent me a note about this and jokingly asked me if I thought that *Mad* was as culturally significant as *National Geographic*. I don't think he expected me to reply with a hearty "Hell yes!" Few magazines captured the national zeitgeist the way that *Mad* did in the '60s and '70s. Want to know what American life was like in 1974? Pick up a contemporary issue of *Mad*. You'll feel the shag carpet beneath your feet before you even reach the *Mad* fold-in on the back cover. During the Nixon era, no other magazine had its finger on the pulse of the country better than *Mad* did, so if you have a pile of them in the attic be sure to keep them along with everything else. The historians and sociologists of tomorrow will thank you.

4

Computers and video games

The best reason to keep old computers is that they're often loaded with things that we don't want other people to see (in some cases they're loaded with things that we *really* don't want other people to see). Computers have replaced so many things. The typewriter, the file cabinet, the photo album, the stash of *Playboys* hidden in the closet—you name it, the computer has replaced it. But as quickly as the home computer shoved all of those things out the door (and hopefully into storage), the computer itself vanished in favor of laptops, iPads, and smartphones. Nowadays, a desktop tower-and-monitor combo is about as uncommon in the American household as a wringer washing machine and a wall-mounted phone. But before we made the quantum leap to portable devices we went through several generations of desk-bound units.

The continuum of computer ownership

- **TRS-80:** The TRS-80 was the 1970s wondermachine that introduced many of us to the space-age glories of high-powered computing. And it was made by RadioShack, which is kind of like if Pep Boys made helicopters. My first awe-inspiring encounter with this science fiction dream-become-reality was typing a few lines of BASIC with my two index fingers and making my name, in glowing green letters, scroll vertically across the screen into infinity. Add another line of code and my name scrolled diagonally! I was suddenly drunk with power, a fourth-grade computer genius. In just a few minutes I grasped more about how computers worked than my parents had learned in their entire lives.

- **Apple II:** Along with the TRS-80, the Apple II was the go-to machine of American schools in the late '70s and early '80s. In my school, computing resources were so scarce that each student was allotted approximately fifteen minutes per semester to do something utterly meaningless, like play a round of *The Oregon Trail*, an allegedly educational text game that sported crude wagon-train graphics and which nearly always ended with grisly death at the

hands of some gross nineteenth century disease.
Mollie Ackerman died of dysentery which, for
me, was pure wish fulfilment. Then I played it
and died of typhoid. On a computer.

- **Commodore VIC-20 and Commodore 64:**
  Many American households were introduced to
  the world of home computing through one of
  these two computers. The Commodore 64 was a
  suped-up—and mega-selling—version of the
  earlier VIC-20 which, itself, was hardly a dud.
  The 64 was infamous for its disc drive which
  was slower than frozen ketchup and sounded like
  a machine gun in a toilet bowl. Both computers
  promised to solve every domestic problem from
  sorting recipes to teaching the kids to read, but
  anyone who owned one knew that they were
  really designed to help you goof off. And that
  recipe-sorting thing is serious. Somehow, early
  computer sales pitches never failed to mention
  recipe-sorting as a major benefit. I suppose it
  makes sense to use a computer to sort your
  recipes, but I wouldn't know because I don't
  cook. Another popular early-computing
  application was *biorhythms,* a pseudoscience that

calculates your lucky and unlucky days based upon your birthdate. It's kind of like a horoscope but without the celestial stuff. Plug in your birthday and you'll instantly know when to avoid the hairdresser and when to play the lottery. Does it work? I still have lousy hair and all of my scratch-off cards paid a big fat zero. So in other words, no, it doesn't. But with a Commodore computer hooked up to your 19" Zenith color TV at least you have the peace of mind of knowing that your biorhythms are only a keystroke away.

- **IBM PC and Macintosh:** And here's where things start to stabilize. The Macintosh was a funny little thing that bundled the computer, disc drive (or *disk* drive if you insist), and a weensie monochrome monitor into a plastic cabinet about the size of a box of saltines. The most remarkable thing about the Macintosh was its nifty on-screen typography which was very un-computer, and when I say un-computer I'm referring to the IBM PC as my basis for comparison. The early PC models (we're talking pre-Windows here, back in the age of DOS when you actually had to know a modicum of computer language to get anything done) also had monochrome monitors, like the Mac, but with glowing green or amber characters on a background of inky blackness, not the newsprint-quality displays that the Macintosh offered. IBMs were workmanlike, not elegant, yet they somehow felt a lot more like a *computer* than the Macintosh did. If the Macintosh was a Rolls Royce, the IBM PC was a pickup truck cobbled together from the parts of twenty-five other vehicles, but it still spun like a top. Well, okay, not always. And once other companies figured out how to duplicate the IBM PC's functionality without violating any patents, we were treated to a flurry of IBM clones, giving rise to a host of machines dubbed *IBM Compatible*. No one bothers to point that out now; it's a given.

And after the IBM PC and Mac came out we enjoyed a few boring decades when the only two types of computers that were available were ever-evolving versions of the Macintosh and the IBM PC. Even so, our closets and basements continue to enshrine the obsolete wonders of the past.

The tripartite computer-retention rationale

There are at least three good reasons to keep your old computers.

1). Access to old software

Nothing sucks harder than firing up your brand-new computer and finding out that all of your favorite games and applications don't work on the latest operating system. If you want to play some of your '80s and '90s favorites, like *Lemmings, Maniac Mansion,* and *Zork,* you're probably out of luck. Your new computer doesn't have a floppy drive; Hell, it probably doesn't even have a CD-drive. You spent all that money on games that you grew to love and now you can't play them. Wouldn't it be nice to spend a few hours with *Myst* or *SimCity* on a lazy weekend afternoon? Of course it would be. Even more essential than games is access to old financial information or written documents. I wrote a zillion things on an ancient word processor called

ProWrite which—*you guessed it*—doesn't work on new computers. One more reason to keep the old ones.

2). Access to old files

Before the age of computers, we kept our photos, homework assignments, lists, and all sorts of other things on pieces of paper. When computers came along we started to store those things on hard drives. Then *the cloud* made its debut and we shuffled all of our snapshots and shopping lists to the limitless expanse of the internet. While this reduced clutter it also created a brand-new problem: Old computers holding old stuff that many of us hadn't thought to port over to our newest device. Since parting with precious family photos and decade-old tax returns is inconceivable to many (thank God) the best solution, naturally, is just to keep the old computer until such time as we see fit to copy and transfer all that stuff. Which we both know is never going to happen.

3). *Denying* access to old files

Of the three great reasons to keep your old computers, this one is the motherlode. Hard drives are filled with sensitive personal information, embarrassing browsing histories, and compromising photographs. You can pull out the hard drive and clobber it to pieces with a hammer. Or you could pour Coca-Cola all over it and let it work its magic (Coca-Cola, given enough time, will allegedly dissolve anything), but it will probably just turn it into a sticky hard drive that will soon be an ant farm. Better to bite the bullet and keep the thing.

If you're serious about using your old computers, remember that old machines don't have USB ports. Monitors, printers, etc. each had their own special, non-universal, non-interchangeable, and occasionally even proprietary, cables. Yay, more things to keep!

The synergy of piling things up

Here's where the beauty of meticulous hoarding truly reveals itself. Firing up an old computer isn't like plugging in your fondue pot. Nope, these beasts typically have several components that you'll have to assemble and coordinate:

- **A computer.** You won't get far without this.

- **A keyboard.** Commodore 64s and a few other family-oriented computers simplified things by having the computer's brain stuffed inside the keyboard, but if you're using an old Mac or PC you'll need to find a keyboard.

- **A monitor or TV set.** In the old days, many of us simply used TV sets in place of monitors, even when dedicated monitors were available. It was a way to save money and make an existing appliance pull double duty. If you're using a TV, you'll have an easier time connecting to an old CRT television with an honest-to-God picture tube in it. Your display would likely be a little wonky on a modern-day flat screen, not to mention that your old computer may have connections that are completely incompatible with newer TVs. Which brings us to...

- **Connector cables.** You'll need cables to connect your old computer to your monitor or TV, and if you're connecting to a flat screen LCD or LED, you'll have to do some hunting to find cables that will bridge the technological changes of the last few decades (no small feat in a world without RadioShack). And you'll also need separate cables to connect your computer to the disc drive, printer, and any other peripherals that you intend to hook up (in the days before USB, computer add-ons often had different unique, mutually incompatible connection cables). Power cords weren't always hardwired, so you may need those, too.

- **Disc drives and tape drives.** Old computers didn't always have disc drives built into the cabinet. You had to purchase them separately and connect them to the computer. And if you're computer is *really* old (or was pitched primarily to the family market) you may need a tape drive, AKA a garden-variety tape recorder that can retrieve computer programs stored on audiocassettes. Does anyone remember tape recorders? Anyone??

- **Printer.** This may come in handy if you need to print out your old high school book reports. But good luck making it work without a new ribbon or ink-jet cartridge. Those things don't last

forever, and replacing them may not be an
option.

- **Game controllers.** If you plan to take a trip
down memory lane with your old video games,
you may also need game controllers, which used
to be single-button joysticks. In other words,
they were simple enough for adults to figure out.

- **Media.** What a bummer it would be if you
carefully pieced together this network of antique
technology only to discover that your mom
threw out all of your old floppy discs (or your
idiot cousin wiped a magnet all over them).
Make sure you have something to *do* with your
old computer before you hook it up.

Once you've assembled all of this, cross your
fingers and switch everything on. Here's hoping that it
all still works!

The most clutterable things about computers

Computers and all of their accompanying cables and peripherals provide enough clutter to warm a hoarder's heart, but the true volume leader among computer clutter is the free CD-ROMs distributed by America Online in the '90s. When online services were new, America Online was the heavyweight champ, and it asserted its dominance by burying the Earth in an infinite barrage of CD-ROMs that promised 500 HOURS FREE! if you signed up right away. If this makes no sense to you, it's probably because A) you're too young to remember a time when you had to buy your internet by the hour, and/or B) you're too young to remember when you needed CD-ROMs to get anything done on a computer. Either way, you're too young to get it. Suffice it to say that America Online mailed CDs to every address on the globe a thousand times over (seriously) and handed them out by the dozen in Walmart checkouts, consuming approximately 12% of the planet's resources in the process. If you still have a pile of these discs, say hello to your chic new coasters

and pocket mirrors, all with a trendy '90s sheen that
your friends will envy.

"Greetings, Program."

All of which brings us to video games. If you're
a child of the seventies (or later) video games are a part
of your life. The games themselves have changed
radically over the years, along with the time that it takes
to play them. I spent three minutes (if I was lucky)
playing *Pac-Man* in the '80s; my daughter spends three
hours playing *Fallout*. Not that I'm judging. I would
gladly have spent three hours playing *Pac-Man*.

In the early years of video gaming, when coin-
operated machines at the grocery store, pizza shop, and
video arcade represented the apex of gaming
technology, manufacturers struggled to bring the fantasy
world of video games directly to the American living
room. It took well over a decade for the homebound
experience to rival what a quarter could buy at the
arcade, but those old home consoles loom large in the
nostalgic recesses of millions of childhoods. Here are a

few that might still lurk in your parents' attic and which, naturally, are too good to throw away:

- ***Pong* consoles:** Some of the first home video games that were designed to take advantage of your TV set, *Pong* clones (mostly unauthorized rip-offs of Atari's coin-operated *Pong* game) allowed you and a friend to bat a point of light back and forth between two "paddles" on an otherwise black screen. Early consoles had the control mounted right on the face of the cabinet, a situation that required uncomfortably close physical proximity to your opponent. More than one cathode-ray tennis match on our 19" Zenith led to real-life hand-to-hand combat between my brother and whichever unlucky friend he suckered into visiting that day. But visit they did, because my brother had a video game which made our house a neighborhood mecca for a brief shining moment circa 1976. *That's what video games did.*

- **Atari 2600:** The workhorse of the early video game years, the Atari 2600 sold approximately one bazillion copies throughout the '70s and '80s. The games themselves were contained on plastic cartridges which had to be plugged into the unit before you could play them on your TV, and the Atari 2600's phenomenal success ensured that there were more cartridges available than it was possible to play in a human lifetime, some of which were based on pretty odd ideas (*Lost Luggage* anyone?). But the phenomenally successful Atari blew it with their lousy home version of *Pac-Man* and a truly painful take on *E.T.: The Extra-Terrestrial*, two games that sucked so badly that they nearly destroyed the entire video game industry and led Atari to dump truckloads of unsold merchandise into a New Mexico landfill in 1983. Sometimes I awaken at night, shaking from a nightmare vision of thousands of beautiful Atari cartridges buried in the cold, hard earth beneath the southwestern desert.

- **Intellivision:** Intellivision, pitched as *intelligent television*, was the snooty, brainy competitor to the scrappy Atari 2600. It was nowhere near as popular as that system was, and it wasn't well suited to action games, but it attracted a devoted following. It's surprising that this game went anywhere given its bizarre handheld controllers which combined a rotating disc with a numeric keypad and four stiff side-mounted buttons, a controller that was such a headscratcher that it has never been duplicated or emulated by any other gaming system.

- **NES (Nintendo Entertainment System):** The gaming system that put home games back on the map after the 1983 crash (see Atari 2600, above). It's famous for popularizing the game *Super Mario Bros.*, which got Mario out from behind Donkey Kong's shadow, and for including a light gun with which players could shoot helpless on-screen waterfowl.

Air it and share it

If you've ever tried to beat your kids over the head (figuratively, of course) with the things that you loved as a child, you probably know how it usually goes: They roll their eyes, go back to their smartphones (which *you* bought and paid for), and leave you embarrassed for bringing up whatever it was you thought they'd like. Shockingly, I've found that this rule often doesn't apply to video games. Healthy initial skepticism aside, the kids are often drawn in by the pared-down structure of many early games and, for once, you may be able to best them at something that they're supposed to be good at. Good luck!

5

Fitness equipment

My husband goes on a semi-annual fitness kick. Our home is littered with the hardware of a thousand fads, regimens, and as-seen-on-TV gizmos, every piece a monument to his failed attempts to tame his Hungry Man TV-dinner physique. *But he means well,* my friends say. Yeah, so did the guy who designed the Titanic.

One day he brought home this godawful-huge rowing machine that he had picked up at a yard sale. He started assembling it in the living room which I had already staked out as the next frontier of my personal Bookshelf Wonderland. I knew as soon as I saw his new clockwork monstrosity that I wanted that damn thing out of the house. Put it in the garage. Put it in the basement. Put it in the back of the pickup. Don't put it in my book space.

But there it was, with my husband pumping away with all of the joy and enthusiasm of a Volga boatman. I knew he hated it, but now it was all about proving a point. He was going to use that gizmo if it killed him (it didn't). After a weekend of scowls, veiled threats, and barely concealed hostility, I tied an extension cord to the front of the machine and dragged it out into the yard. Then I blocked his next move: I filled the living room with piles of books before he got home from work. Just before that magic moment arrived, I had an epiphany. I hooked up the lawn sprinkler and hauled it over to the rowing machine. Now he could enjoy a refreshing "ocean" spray while he grunted through his routine, happily out of sight, out of earshot, and out of the living room.

Completely in character, my husband admitted defeat and went back to his couch-sitting ways for another six months or so. I know he was relieved that he no longer had to pay lip service to physical fitness, but the bug would bite him again and the cycle would begin anew. In the meantime, the rowing machine is out in the yard. We'll move it to the shed right after we take down the Christmas lights that we hung from the roof in 2006.

Don't get me wrong, I'm happy to pile up exercise equipment. I have no objection to creating the illusion that we're health-conscious and non-sedentary. My issues all have to do with space allocation. There's also the problem of residential structural integrity. I knew something was up when I spilled a carton of Whoppers on the dining room table and they rolled together in a group, onto the floor, and across the room like a herd of chocolatey lemmings. As the dogs chowed down on malted milk I gazed suspiciously at the dusty mountain of free weights and dumbbells that were stacked in front of the china cabinet. The floor wasn't level and it surely wasn't because the house was 150 years old and the foundation had settled. Nope, it was those damn free weights. They had to go.

So it was settled. My husband's glorified paperweights had no business in the dining room. They belonged in the kitchen or the TV room or the bedroom or the bathroom. The dining room was for books. I hauled him off the couch and we just about killed ourselves lugging what I swear was a truckload of thousand-pound weights up two flights of stairs to the attic which is partially converted to living space. Afterward, while we sprawled on the floor in a sweaty heap, I noticed little popping and cracking sounds coming from the pile of weights. Was it smart to stack them right above the master bedroom? I called my architect friend to ask his advice and he recommended that we remove the weights from the attic IMMEDIATELY. It turns out that most attic floors aren't built to the same standard as the floors in the residential parts of the house and that anyone who would store things like boulders and safes and anvils and *free weights* up there is an idiot. Who knew? So off we went, dragging an endless pile of cast iron down three flights of stairs to the basement. Why we didn't just take them down there to begin with I couldn't tell you, but I think it had something to do with my husband's fantasy of actually using the weights if they were in the attic. As if. He can pump iron in the basement if he feels the itch. It's cooler down there anyway.

Around the world on a stationary bike

My husband has a bicycle. It's a nice one, a Schwinn. I think. Well, it was expensive. And he never rides it. It's in the shed with two flat tires. It was this little detail which led me to object to his planned purchase of a stationary bike. "If you don't ride the bike you have," I said, "Why on God's green Earth would you ride one that doesn't even go anywhere?"

Naturally, he had a list of reasons:

- The great indoors are air conditioned.

- He can watch his old *Seinfeld* DVDs while he pedals to nowhere.

- He can play music without wearing earbuds (which he insists don't fit in his ears due to a bizarre genetic defect known only to him).

- He can sweat with impunity.

- He can wear whatever he likes and not have to pass muster with the fitness-fashion mafia.

- I don't have to worry about him ogling a roomful of spandex-clad beauties.

That last one was written just for me. I'm sure he thought it would cut right through all of my objections, but he really didn't have to try so hard. I fall for his fitness schemes every time: If he insists he'll use it, I agree to the purchase. Then, a month later, we're looking for a new home for our latest pricey white elephant.

He wound up buying an exercycle that has a little video screen that gives the rider a first-person view of Paris, London, Hong Kong, etc., providing the illusion of cycling through the world's most glamorous cities. It sounds pretty cool, but in practice it's more like a slide-show. I told my husband that it would have made better sense if they had made it look as though he was cycling through the aisles of Walmart, with the option to purchase the items as he passed by. He thought this was the greatest idea ever and resolved to carry this message directly to Jeff Bezos. So now I know whom to blame if this technology ever rears its ugly head.

When to pull the plug

I devised an ingenious method to discover when the latest exercise-machine fetish has reached its conclusion. I call it *The B-cup Strategem*: I hang a bra on one of the handlebars. If two weeks go by and it hasn't moved then I know that my husband has grown bored and it's time to drag the contraption out into the yard. In this last case, it took about a month and a half, which may be a personal best. And to that I can only add that the exercycle makes an awesome garden-tool caddy.

6

—

Movies and music

1996 was a glorious year for accumulators. Prior to 1996, the movie fans among us—and who doesn't like movies?—had to build our movie collections out of VHS tapes (or out of LaserDiscs if we were snotty elitists, or out of Betamax tapes if we were stubborn early adopters who didn't know when to admit defeat). Some of us built awesome libraries out of those clunky videotapes, but in 1996 movie collecting changed forever: 1996 was when DVDs arrived at Walmart.

I was skeptical at first. Were DVDs really that much better than videocassettes? And what good was a DVD if I couldn't use it to tape tonight's episode of *Friends?*

But, like the rest of us, it wasn't long before I caught the DVD bug, and then a wondrous thing happened: I started buying movies faster than I could watch them. A *lot* faster. **If buyer's remorse has a polar opposite, this was it: I had buyer's *euphoria*.** I couldn't scarf them up fast enough. And then complete seasons of TV shows started coming out and I had to buy *those*. I still have DVDs from those heady early days that have never seen the inside of a player, but I promise that one day I'll get around to watching all fourteen seasons of *Dallas.* Just you wait!

Keeping it real: The case for physical media

Our music collections have undergone similar evolutions, from LPs, to reel-to-reels, to 8-track tapes and cassettes, to shiny CDs. I think I have *Sgt. Pepper's* on every format and probably *The Dark Side of the Moon,* too. Like the music-obsessed Rob Gordon in Nick Hornby's *High Fidelity,* I can look at my collection and know just what was going on in my life when I bought each album and listened to each tune. I remember dozing off in the back seat of my dad's Buick Riviera while the Bee Gees hit their upper registers in "How Deep Is Your Love," and putting the finishing touches on an eighth-grade science project while Fleetwood Mac spun in the background. Every time I see one of those old records I'm taken back to an earlier time in my life, and it feels good.

You used to be able to tell a lot about someone by gazing over their music collection. If it was all Leif Garret, Bay City Rollers, and Shaun Cassidy, you were dealing with a teenybopper. If it was full of James

Taylor, Bread, and Gilbert O'Sullivan, then the owner was a whiny white guy. A shelf full of Foghat, Grand Funk Railroad, and Bachman Turner Overdrive could only be owned by a badass (or a badass wannabe). And if there were Percy Sledge, Barry White, and Luther Vandross albums on the coffee table, you were about to get laid.

Sadly, downloading and streaming have closed this window into the souls of others and replaced it with… nothing. There are no more grubby cassettes in our cars, no piles of sun-baked 8-tracks in our dens, no stacks of scuffed-up LPs by our bedsides. Instead we have digital files which leave no physical trace. The flea-market hounds of the future will come up empty handed when they go digging around for the top hits of 2019.

LPs: An object lesson in holding on

When I started buying my own music my format of choice was cassette (I already had a couple of 8-tracks that my parents had bought for me—the *Star*

Wars soundtrack and ELO's *Discovery*—but those don't count because I didn't pay for them). I rapidly switched over to LPs when I learned that they had better sound quality, a full square-foot (or more) of space for awesome album art, and sometimes really cool tchotchkes, like posters or stickers, tucked inside. Then CDs came out, with their crystal-clear sound and virtual indestructability, and LPs vanished from the record stores like pork rinds at a tractor pull. A year or two later the cassette tapes disappeared and then it was all CDs all the time for years and years and years. Streaming and downloading (remember Napster?) took a huge bite out of CDs and, as of 2019, it looks like they're on the way out, too. But guess what's back and all the rage?

LPs! Just as movies and music move increasingly to digital-only options, LPs came roaring back from oblivion. And it isn't just the trendy millennials buying them. They sell LPs at Target for crying out loud! The significance of this can't be overstated. It's like bringing back corded phones, or swapping our laptops for typewriters. When you find yourself tempted to dump your obsolete treasures, just remember, the **people who saved their LPs instead of**

selling them at yard sales went from hoarders to hipsters in the blink of an eye.

Back to video: double dipping DVDs

The true pinnacle of movie collecting is the phenomenon known as *double dipping:* buying the same title multiple times because they keep adding little tweaks and improvements to it. It goes without saying that I had to replace my old Vestron VHS tape of *Dirty Dancing* with a shiny new DVD version, but little did I know that I'd experience the joy of replacing that DVD just a few short years later with an *even better* DVD version, with remastered picture and exclusive new bonus features; and *then* with a "Special Edition" DVD with even more new bonus features; and *then* with an "Ultimate Edition" DVD with even *more* new stuff (or old stuff—how could I pass up the chance to own *Dirty Dancing: Live in Concert?);* and *then* they came up with a version that came packed with a book (they know my weakness); and *then* it debuted on a newfangled blu-ray disc and we started all over again.

And in this continuum of *Dirty Dancing* we see the beauty of video collecting: thanks to the selfless resourcefulness of the movie studios we get to buy the same movies over and over again. It's wonderful that someone gets to take our money by enabling obsessive-compulsive collectors who can't say no to the latest iteration of *Top Gun*. And don't even get me started on *Star Wars*.

Now I have to admit that, after a while, even I became frustrated by the sheer volume of movies piling up on my shelves. When something's gotta give something's gotta give, but I just couldn't bring myself to part with anything that was already in my collection. That's when I discovered the magic of consolidating all editions of any given movie inside a single DVD case. I can easily slip an old DVD into a paper envelope (you can buy them at Walmart) and then stick the disc-and-envelope inside the case with the newer version of the movie, and then throw the old case away. There is almost always enough room to cram one or two extra discs in a case (with DVDs anyhow; blu-ray cases are smaller and sometimes you really have to do some shoehorning to make it work), but when the reissues get out of control, as with *Dirty Dancing,* you'll find yourself testing the structural limits of those little plastic cases (Trivia: those plastic DVD cases are called "keep cases." I should have told you that before). If I have to shove four or more discs into a case it may be time to explore alternative solutions. While I think there's something charming about seeing my bursting *Dirty Dancing* case held together by rubber bands, there is a better way.

Bound together

As much as I love to display my movies for all the world to see (like showing off my epic collection of *Police Academy* films), there comes a time when I simply have to come to a reckoning with the fact that what those black plastic DVD cases mostly hold is air. Here's a way to make more efficient use of that space and make room for even more movies.

1. Your neighborhood discount store sells binders filled with pockets designed to hold 5" optical discs (AKA CDs and DVDs). Go buy one.

2. Use a white laundry marker to number the pockets one to whatever.

3. Take the discs out of their cases and put them into the numbered pockets.

4. Set up a simple Excel spreadsheet and enter the disc titles and their corresponding pocket numbers.

Voilà! You just cleared a mile of shelf space without sacrificing a single movie to yard-sale oblivion, *and* you have a spreadsheet to help you locate every movie in your collection. The only drawback is that movies relegated to *The Album* will suffer from out-of-sight, out-of-mind syndrome: If you weren't watching them when you could see them on the shelf, you sure as hell aren't going to watch them when they're stashed away in an album.

Wait: What about VHS?

If you're thinking about trashing all of your old videocassettes, remember that there are a few important movies that were released years ago on VHS that have *never* transitioned to DVD or any other digital format. The Beatles' 1970 movie *Let it Be* hasn't seen the light of day since it was released on VHS and LaserDisc in 1982. If you have one of those, count your lucky stars and don't get rid of it.

As revolutionary as VHS was, ushering in the home-video era, it was a terrible format. Right out of the box the picture was fuzzy and streaked, and it doesn't get better with age. VHS tapes deteriorate even if you never pop them into a machine. So why save them? There is an active videocassette nostalgia community that treasures pre-Photoshop VHS box art which was often striking and imaginative, and the lo-fi video and audio that evoke rainy childhood afternoons and popcorn-filled family movie nights. To me, this makes about as much sense as getting misty-eyed over fold-up road maps when I have a GPS app on my phone—it's about the movie, not the format. But who am I to judge another's nostalgic hoarding? God knows that I do enough of it, and believe me, my husband knows, too.

Nostalgic for fitness; or, fitness nostalgia

Unearthing old VHS tapes can set in motion chains of events the ends of which no one can anticipate. A friend of mine, in an ill-advised bout of decluttering her rumpus room, unearthed an old Bartles & Jaymes wine-cooler case filled with forgotten videocassettes from the era of *ALF* and *Max Headroom*. I'm sure she experienced something of the thrill of Indiana Jones liberating the fabled Ark of the Covenant from its dusty tomb as she lifted a worn copy of *Jane Fonda's Workout* from its home between *Dorf on Golf* and *Making Michael Jackson's Thriller*. Inspired, she hooked up the old family VCR and excavated her neon-pink leotard and leg warmers, also fortuitously preserved. When her husband returned from an all-consuming mission to Pep Boys to find his wife sweating away in her '80s workout gear, well, it was more than the poor man could handle.

Nine months later they welcomed a fresh new addition to the family and they've lived happily ever after, with that fateful copy of *Jane Fonda's Workout* elevated to a place of honor among their other precious family treasures.

The wonder of early camcorder

Your old videocassettes may be outclassed but they still hold a charm that only antiquity (or obsolescence) can bequeath. That isn't just a thirty-year-old copy of *Lady and the Tramp* in a white clamshell case, that was your little sister's best friend for eight months in 1987. And the tape has tiny Spaghetti-O fingerprints to prove it.

And on that sentimental note, let's dwell for a moment on all of the home movies that you haven't looked at in twenty years. In this age of instant streaming video, of YouTube and Instagram, it's hard to remember a time when home movies were a precious commodity, something that took effort and foresight to produce and that, in most cases, existed only in a single, treasured copy. They couldn't be shared with the world; they couldn't go viral. They were viewed by small groups of family and friends on special occasions and then carefully tucked away on a shelf where, like your photo albums, they represented a tangible archive of family history. Over the years, as technology improved, those movies, whether they were on videocassettes or reels of Super-8 film, were shunted aside and forgotten. Many of my own have become lost and currently top the list of "most-wanted household objects" right above my favorite corkscrew and the third replacement TV remote.

Somewhere in my home there's a box filled with the records of birthday parties, weddings, family vacations, playtime with pets, and other episodes of daily life, both extraordinary and commonplace. Here, hidden away in little spools of magnetic tape, is a world where my parents will always be young, where my sister is still a brat, where my first dog waits to greet me after school, and where beloved family members, long departed, still gather to wish me happy birthday.

Pro tips

- **Keep your videocassettes rewound and store them vertically on their narrow edges.** A tight tape is a happy tape and keeping your cassettes rewound maintains tension on the spool so that things don't get saggy. Don't store them flat. Storing them flat causes the tape to curl up like the letter C, and that's not good. Keep them rewound and store them vertically like books.

- **Store LPs and other vinyl records vertically.** Storing them horizontally increases the chances of warpage, especially to the platters on the bottom of a heavy stack. And some of you young 'uns may need a reminder that vinyl records must be kept away from high heat and direct sunlight. That'll warp 'em for sure!

- **Even better, convert them to DVDs or some other digital format.** It's the 21st century. It's time. Videocassettes degrade; DVDs and CDs apparently do as well, but I have yet to see one that shows signs of wearing out. You can and should keep your originals, but hire a conversion service or buy a DVD/VCR combo deck and switch those tapes to digital. Or skip the DVD and just have them converted to digital video files. Personally, I go for the DVDs. I prefer things that take up space.

7

Toys

I spent hours with Barbie and Ken, dressing them in flashy fashions and speeding them away in their pink convertible (with 8-track player) for a dream date at the supermarket; setting up Holly Hobbie in her general store right out of *Little House on the Prairie;* and sitting on the carpet while scrawling mind-bending patterns with plastic cogwheels from my Spirograph set. Then I grabbed my keys and went to work.

A white-hot connection to childhood

All across the nation, flea markets and yard sales crawl with people trying to recapture a little piece of childhood by collecting the toys that they had when they were kids. The obvious solution to this problem is to just *keep* the toys you already had, but most of our parents threw them out the minute we left home. Since they're the ones who paid for them you'd think they'd be a little more reluctant to get rid of them, especially since many are now worth a small fortune. (Remember how Mollie Ackerman's vacation was paid for? I sure do).

Not that I would sell them. On the contrary, I'd rather keep them around. Opening a box that's been packed since childhood is like a trip back in time. Memories come rushing back, and people long forgotten reappear before us, along with all of the associated emotions, as if they themselves had been packed up with cardboard and tape. Maybe it was your sixth birthday; maybe it was an afternoon spent with your best friend in the den; or maybe, like me, it was an epic fight with your sister over who got to play with the Easy-Bake Oven. Easy-Bake Ovens have sharp corners and getting banged in the head with a miniature version of a major appliance is no fun. But I won the fight and my wailing sister went off to her corner while I replaced the oven's 100-watt bulb and baked a chocolate cake. Which I gleefully gobbled up in front of her. All these years later I can still taste the sweetness of victory.

My brothers also liked to beat the crap out of each other with toys, but they preferred to do it with wiffle bats and roller skates. They also enjoyed proxy combat in the form of Rock 'Em Sock 'Em Robots, a game of legendary physical durability. My brothers broke a lot of toys, but the Rock 'Em Sock 'Em Robots always came out unscathed.

Some toys are hard to keep

Many parents threw out their kids' toys after
they left home, fostering a sense of betrayal that
sometimes rears its ugly head at Thanksgiving and
funerals and other family get-togethers. My parents,
though, were loath to dispose of any of their offspring's
treasured playthings. They were sensitive like that. Or
maybe they had four kids and understood the economic
benefits of hand-me-downs. Either way, I am blessed
with boxes of plastic gadgets that were developed by
America's most brilliant minds to provide for the
amusement of their progeny (and to keep them quiet
when the neighbors came over for pinochle).

Two of the most insidious toys developed by 20th
century science were Silly Putty and Slime, both
chemical compounds of limited play value that found
permanent homes deep inside countless living room
carpets (Play-Doh was just as bad, but at least you could
make things with it and it tasted good). Slime pretty
much came as advertised. It was a wad of green gunk

that came in a plastic trash can, and there was precious little you could do with it other than make a mess, make fart noises, and knead it into the carpet. *Genius.* Unfortunately, Slime tended to dry up into something that resembled clotted mucous. Even if you managed to save some (which I hope you did), by now it's probably transmogrified into a nasty crust.

Silly Putty was slightly more interesting. It came in a little plastic egg and you could roll it into a ball, bounce it, stretch it, transfer mirror images from the funny pages, take molds of your fingerprints, and knead it into the carpet. *Genius.* When I pounded a glob of Silly Putty into our bright-red deep-pile living-room shag, my mother's face turned a hue that just about matched, if not surpassed, the crimson shade of the rug. She handed me a butter knife and I spent the next hour scraping every last molecule of Silly Putty out of those synthetic fibers. At the end of this process I held a noxious mixture of Silly Putty, red carpet shavings, dirt, and hair that just about made me puke (I probably would have, but I didn't want to clean up another mess). My mother told me to keep it because it was the last Silly Putty I would ever own. I tossed it, of course, but I also proved my mother wrong: They still make Silly Putty and I have a wad of it on my shelf as I write this. Way to predict the future, Mom!

Thanks to the ever-spinning wheel of nostalgia, toys that we thought were long gone keep returning to store shelves. During a recent trip to Target I was thrilled to see that Stretch Armstrong has been reincarnated for the 21st century. Stretch Armstrong is a soft, rubbery muscle man that can be stretched to unhealthy proportions, pounded flatter than a pancake, tied up in knots, you name it. The toy is downright bizarre (which made it particularly appropriate to its original era in the 1970s) and everyone wondered what secrets lay beneath Stretch's silky-smooth dermis. In a seizure of spiteful curiosity, I took scissors to my brother's toy (he was bored with it anyway) and sliced it open. Imagine my wonder and surprise when *corn syrup* oozed from the laceration. And that explains Stretch Armstrong's short shelf life. The components just don't hold up over the years and many specimens from the toy's heyday have disintegrated into a sickening soup. If you packed one away, I sure hope it's in the *bottom* of the box. Anyhow, now that Stretch Armstrong has returned, maybe I'll slice one open above a stack of pancakes. The kids will love it!

All the toys you *should* have kept

Thanks to my retentive parents (and three follow-on siblings) my family still has many old playthings that were passed down to succeeding generations. Especially treasured are old Fisher-Price Play Family sets, the ones with the wooden characters that are precisely shaped and sized to plug up a toddler's throat. Safety hazards aside, these longtime staples of church-basement nurseries have a certain *je ne sais quoi* that the newer Fisher-Price sets (they call those characters *Little People* now) just can't muster. These and myriad other toys were played with, cared for, and preserved in my parents' home across the span of four childhoods. With the exception of a few favorites that I've taken into my own custody, that's where they remain, all of their joy and wonder waiting to be discovered by a new generation.

The toys that we played with years ago are often worth money today. They're worth more money when they're left in their original packages, pristine and unopened. Open them anyway. Play with them, get them dirty, wear them out, squeeze every last bit of joy out of them. That's where their true worth resides. What are they worth to *you?*

Conclusion: The life-changing magic of piling things up

A few weeks ago, my mother dropped by for a visit.
She had warned me that she was coming; it wasn't a
surprise. This meant that I had to "clean" the house. I
saw to it that there was a clear path to the bathroom and
enough room on the sofa for an extra person. As soon as
she arrived I could tell that something was up. She was
tense, nervous, furtive, and I didn't think it was because
of the stack of books on the coffee table that towered
over her head when she sat down.

Over the next fifteen minutes my sister, a
brother, and two of my friends filed into my living
room, struggling to find places to plant themselves
among all of the junk that I'd left scattered around. *This
was an intervention.* As I kept a wary eye on my guests I
gathered the vodka and the rum and the gin and the wine
and the vermouth and the tequila and the whiskey and
the schnapps and moved them all to safekeeping. Then
my mother spoke.

"Honey, we've been talking and we're worried
about you. Isn't it time to consider thinking about
beginning to take some baby steps toward possibly
putting together a plan to start contemplating maybe,
you know, letting a few of your things go? On a trial
basis?"

I really appreciated the fact that these people, all of whom I love unconditionally, took the time and made the effort to come to my home for the sole purpose of helping me to live a better life. I took a moment to gather my thoughts and sensitively replied, "Are you freaking *kidding* me?" I looked to my sister. "What was your favorite toy when you were a kid?"

"My Holly Hobbie doll," she said.

"And where is that doll now?"

"I don't know."

"I do. It's in the landfill. Do you know what *my* favorite toys were?"

"The Sunshine Family?"

"Yes! And do you know where they are now?"

She rolled her eyes. "Somewhere in this house obviously."

"You better believe it. They're in the closet at the end of the hall and I can get them out and set them back up in their plastic '70s hippie commune any time I damn well feel like it." I turned to my brother, who

looked like he wanted to sink into the chair and vanish.
"And you. Where are your *Star Wars* toys?"

"Good question. Where are my *Star Wars* toys,
Mom?"

I could see the panic brewing in my mother's
mind as the situation slipped beyond her control.
"Honey, I don't think your brother and sister came here
to talk about their toys."

One of my friends offered her two cents. "You
had *Star Wars* toys? Did you have the radio-controlled
R2-D2?"

My brother's eyes lit up. "Oh my God yes! I
loved that!"

"So did I! I used to sleep with it at night. Then
one day my parents cleaned out my room and it was
gone. I mean, who didn't love R2-D2? I wish I still had
it."

Now my mother's co-conspirators were
animatedly discussing their favorite lost toys while my
mother, defeated, collapsed back into the couch (or
would have if there hadn't been a pile of dog toys on the
cushion behind her). I walked to the hall closet to

retrieve the heavy artillery, the multi-part *pièce de résistance* that I knew would forever turn the tide of battle in my favor and bring me sweet, sweet victory.

When I returned to the room with a column of boxes stacked up to my chin, my guests stared in slackjawed wonder at what I carried. I carefully placed the cardboard tower on the floor, wiped the junk off of the coffee table with a graceful sweep of my arm, and spread out Hungry Hungry Hippos, Simon, Mousetrap, Ants in the Pants, Concentration, Digital Derby, and a host of other forgotten games of our '70s and '80s childhoods.

"You have Simon! Does it still work?"

"I love Hungry Hungry Hippos!"

"I had Mousetrap, but I broke all the pieces!"

I smiled in gloating triumph. "Which one should we play first? And don't worry about making a mess. Believe me, I won't even notice."

We spent the next few hours gleefully proving my point: It's better to keep than it is to let go. When I look around at all that I've accumulated, every little bit of it sparks joy.

As the group said their goodbyes at the end of a long, fun evening, my mother turned to me, still concerned. "I know you love all of this, Katrina, but you would have such a nice home if it wasn't packed so full of *things*."

"I do have a nice home. It's a *wonderful* home and all of these things that fill it are what make it that way. And here. I have something for you." I pulled a small, heavy glass object from a wrinkly paper bag and handed it to her.

My mother turned it in her hands, speechless. It was my dad's after shave decanter, a glass bottle in the shape of a VW Beetle, part of a series that Avon sold back in the 1970s. She finally spoke, her voice a whisper. "I can't believe you still have this."

"Open it," I said.

She pulled the plastic fender from the back of the miniature glass car and unscrewed the cap that it concealed. She hesitated. Then she brought the bottle to her nose and inhaled. In that moment, forty years vanished. She was young again, her children were playing in the backyard, and the love of her life was in the next room waiting for her to join him for a short while before putting the kids to bed.

She replaced the screwcap and wiped her dampened eyes. "I'm so glad you kept this," she said. "Thank you." She handed it back to me. I pressed it to her palm.

"You came here to talk me into downsizing all of this," I said, waving my arm at the clutter that surrounded us. "I think I can let that piece go. You keep it." She smiled, we embraced, and I closed the door behind her as she followed my siblings down the driveway, calling after them to look at what I had given her. What a marvelous evening it had turned out to be.

Treasure your possessions. Don't give in to the pressure to dispose of the things you worked hard to acquire. You may be happier with them than without them. My mantra is a simple one:

I love it.

I earned it.

I'm keeping it forever.

I only hope I never have to move.

About the authors

Katrina Karapandi has a curator's eye and a hoarder's heart. She scours junk shops and estate sales throughout the Hudson Valley in a noble quest to eliminate the unoccupied space in her home.

Jason Liller is an author, editor, ghostwriter, book consultant, and literary surgeon who works with everyone from first-time writers to bestselling authors whose names he thinks you would recognize. He lives in Pennsylvania with his wife, daughter, and two beautiful dogs. Contact Jason at Jason@LillerCreative.com.